Quick Career

Solutions

Destiny S. Harris

. . .

. . .

Copyright

. . .

. . .

A Gift For You

Thank you for taking the time to read this book. As a token of my appreciation, here is a gift to you.

I give away free books daily. Here's how to get your free books today:

Step 1: Visit amazon.com/author/destinyharris

Step 2: Filter books by "Price: Low to High"

Step 3: Download available free eBooks

. . .

. . .

Table of Contents

...

. . .

Quick Bit

Thank you for taking the time to read this book.

My hope is that you leave at least 1% better than before you read this book and walk away with at least one takeaway.

I'd like to graciously ask that you help me by leaving a <u>review</u> of this book; your feedback helps me write better books and helps others get a glimpse of the book.

With Kindness,
Destiny

...

. . .

#1 Intentions

Set your intention.

1. What position do you desire?

2. Describe your ideal work culture.

3. Describe your ideal co-workers and boss.

4. When do you plan to acquire this new role?

5. How much do you want the position to pay?

. . .

. . .

#2 Requirements

What background, experience, education, and certifications are needed to obtain this role?

If you don't meet all the requirements, don't allow this to stop you from applying.

There are many unqualified people in quality roles.

If there is anything you can do in the meantime to meet more requirements, do what you have to do so you give hiring teams less reason to hesitate or say "no" to your candidacy.

. . .

. . .

#3 Communicating Confidence

Interviewing is about skills and experience, but it's mostly about confidence and demonstrating you can be successful and solve problems in the role you're trying to attain.

If you lack healthy communication and confidence, start practicing now.

Fake it until you make it, and conduct as many mock interviews as you have time for so you can become a master of interviewing.

. . .

. . .

#4 Ruthlessly Apply

Some people can get an interview and a job off a few applications. But many folks need to apply and submit many applications steadily.

The best way to get a job is to apply daily and submit plenty of applications.

Every job application submitted is another lead. The more leads you put out, the more interviews you get. The more interview opportunities you get, the more likely you will close in on an offer.

How many apps should you submit? The choice is up to you. There have been people who submit 1-3 applications daily and others who submit 300 applications daily.

. . .

. . .

#5 The Resume

A resume is never complete until you sign the offer. Continue optimizing your resume based on the job descriptions of the jobs you apply to and the new skills and knowledge you acquire throughout the application process.

By the time you sign an offer, your resume should be stellar perfection.

...

. . .

#6 Don't Get Emotional

You will experience rejection. Many times, hiring teams won't even tell you why.

Don't take it personally.

When you receive a rejection, apply for another job.

Keep your energy high and stay focused on applying. Never get phased by "no".

Frequently, I get excited about receiving a "no" because I know that means I'm a step closer to a "yes."

Keep applying, and don't get attached to any company until you sign the offer.

. . .

. . .

#7 Never Stop Interviewing

Never stop interviewing, even if you're 100% happy with your job. Stay in the market. Stay on top of trends. Keep your interview skills fresh and ready.

Consistently interviewing keeps your candidacy competitive and also keeps your options open.

Complacency is the biggest destroyer of careers. People rarely tap into their unlimited career potential because they get "comfortable" too quickly.

Keep applying. Stay in the market.

. . .

. . .

Thank You For Reading

Thank you for reading this book.

Stay loved, blessed, lucky, favored, aware, joyous, enlightened, and committed to bettering yourself.

. . .

. . .

The End.

. . .

. . .

About Destiny S. Harris

Destiny S. Harris' goal is to positively inspire, cultivate, elevate, and educate the minds of individuals across the globe through her writing.

Creating (whether books, courses, articles, poetry, or music) has always been Destiny's thing, not to mention health & fitness and all things entrepreneurial.

Destiny published her first book, "Beauty Secrets for Girls," at age 11 and her second book, "Don't Wait Until It's Too Late," at age 12.

Destiny obtained three degrees in Psychology, Political Science, & Women's Studies. She also started her own music teaching business at the age of 14, which she led for over ten years. In addition, she has been teaching academic, career, and personal development topics to thousands of students and readers since 2004.

Outside of writing, Destiny loves and enjoys many activities: reading, weightlifting, walking, biking, traveling, football (and sports in general), dogs, animals, food, classic movies, quality and new experiences, mountain and ocean views, sleeping, plants, and nature.

Check out her work, leave a review, share your thoughts with your friends and family, and participate in a movement: **Serving others through self-education (books).**

Complete the Steps To Get Free eBooks:

Step 1: Go to amazon.com/author/destinyharris

Step 2: Filter books by "Price: Low to High"

Step 3: Download available free books

. . .

. . .

Connect W/ Destiny S. Harris

Please reach out and stay in touch. Start a conversation today @ destinyh.com

...

. . .

Free Gifts!

Access courses & free eBooks at the link below:

destinyh.com

. . .

Please Leave A Review

If this book impacts you in some way, please let me know by dropping a review on it.

I write better books with **your** input.

. . .

Tell Me What You Want

I've written many books, but if you don't see what you're looking for or need, get in touch with me via my website, articles, comments, or reviews, and let me know what you're looking for so I can create it for you. I'm here to serve.

Destiny

. . .

...